Copyright ©2021 By Molly Bond All rights reserved.

Legal & Disclaimer

The information contained in this book and its contents is not designed to replace or take the place of any form of medical or professional advice; and is not meant to replace the need for independent medical, financial, legal or other professional advice or services, as may be required. The content and information in this book has been provided for educational and entertainment purposes only.

The content and information contained in this book has been compiled from sources deemed reliable, and it is accurate to the best of the Author's knowledge, information and belief. However, the Author cannot guarantee its accuracy and validity and cannot be held liable for any errors and/or omissions. Further, changes are periodically made to this book as and when needed. Where appropriate and/or necessary, you must consult a professional (including but not limited to your doctor, attorney, financial advisor or such other professional advisor) before using any of the suggested remedies, techniques, or information in this book.

CONTENTS

INTRODUCTION 5

CLASSIC BREAKFAST SANDWICH RECIPES 7

Creamy Brie Pancake Sandwich 7

Hot Pork Sausage And Srambled Egg Sandwich 8

Chocolate Hazelnut French Toast Panini 9

Mediterranean Sandwich 10

Pork Sandwiches..11

Prosciutto And Pesto Panini 12

Ultimate Blt Melt 13

Gruyere, Apple And Ham Sandwich..14

Classic Egg, Ham And Cheese 15

Croissant Sandwich With Sausage, Egg, And Cheddar 16

Classic Grilled Cheese Sandwich 17

Buffalo Patty Melt Panini 18

Olive And Cheese Snack 19

Peanut Butter Waffle With Banana 20

Maple Bacon Waffle Sandwich 21

Red Pepper And Goat Cheese Sandwich 22

Almond Flour Waffle And Sausage Sandwich 23

The Thanksgiving Turkey Cuban Panini 24

Chocolate Croissant..25

Crunchy Nutella And Strawberry Bagel 26

Mexican-style Egg And Beans Sandwich 27

Sausage & Gravy Biscuit..28

Ham And Relish Melt 29

Ground Turkey Taco Cups..30

Sour Cream And Crab Cake Sandwich 31

Eggs Benedict With Ham 32

Prosciutto And Egg Bagel Panini 33

Taleggio And Salami Panini With Spicy Fennel Honey 34

Buffalo Chicken Panini 35

Bacon Egg And Sausage Breakfast Panini 36

The Ham & Cheese 37

Lemony Delicious Summer Vegetable Panini 38

Avocado Sandwich With Egg, Ham And Cheese 39

Chipotle Chicken Sandwich 40

Bacon Mozzarella, Zucchini And Tomato Panini 41

Peanut Butter Bagel Sandwich 42

Spinach, Parmesan And Egg White 43

Pressed Turkey Sandwich 44

Choco-coconut Nut Quesadilla 45

Smoked Salmon And Brie Sandwich 46

The Ultimate Chicken, Spinach And Mozzarella Sandwich 47

Mixed Berry French Toast Panini 48

Eggs Benedict Sandwich 49

Tomato, Egg And Avocado 50

Turkey Salsa Melt 51

Spicy Sandwich 52

Apple Pie Sandwich 53

Italian Egg Whites On Ciabatta 54

Ham And Cheese Egg Biscuit Sandwich 55

Almond Pancake With Egg And Prosciutto 56

Shaved Asparagus And Balsamic Cherries With Pistachios Panini 57

Chili Sandwich 58

Piña Colada Croissant 59

Sausage Omelet With Paprika And Cheese 60

Muffuletta Breakfast Sandwich..61

Quick And Easy Quesadillas 62

Prosciutto And Fig Panini 63

Provolone Baby Mushroom And Caramelized Onion Panini 64

Fried Egg And Cheese Bagel...65

Corn Bowl With Tomato, Bacon, And Cheese 66

Parmesan And Bacon On Whole Wheat..67

Southwest Quesadilla...68

Spinach Havarti Sandwich...69

Apple And Brie Croissant Sandwich..70

Ground Beef Sandwich Pitas..71

Cheesy Chicken Waffle Sandwich...72

Caramel Cashew Waffle Sandwich..73

Salsa And Shrimp Biscuit Sandwich...74

Ratatouille Panini..75

Mushroom & Swiss Bagel..76

Pancake, Sausage & Egg Sandwich...77

Classic Italian Cold Cut Panini...78

Bacon Cheddar And Tomato Panini..79

Feta Lamb And Babba Ghanoush Panini..80

Beef, Waffle, And Egg Sandwich..81

Beef And Veggies Bagel Sandwich..82

Pesto Beef And Mozzarella Panini..83

Cuban Sandwich..84

Chocolate Donut Dessert Sandwich...85

Almond Butter & Honey Biscuit...86

Egg Whites With Mozzarella...87

Peach Basil Croissant...88

Blueberry Marshmallow Sandwich...89

Mexican Gluten-free Pork Sandwich..90

Salmon And Pistachio Melt...91

The Ultimate 4-minute Cheeseburger...92

Bacon Date Sandwich..93

Veggie And Pork Mayo Sandwich...94

Eggs Florentine Biscuit..95

Breakfast Pizza Sandwich..96

RECIPES INDEX...**97**

INTRODUCTION

You've probably seen the commercials for the magical breakfast sandwich makers that, within five minutes or so, depending on the brand of sandwich maker, makes you a delicious breakfast sandwich that rivals the fast food joint with the golden arches. I hate making breakfast every morning, but I know how important it is and this gadget made it look so simple. So, my 12-year-old and I gave the breakfast sandwich maker a try.

How breakfast sandwich makers work
Using a breakfast sandwich maker is just as simple as the commercials make it look. You put a slice of bread in, add cheese and/or pre-cooked meat, slide the egg barrier in, crack an egg onto the egg barrier, top with another slice of bread and close.

Sandwiches in a snap
I tried the machine first and forgot to put the bread on top twice because I got distracted. This caused the egg to dribble out the side of the machine. No problem! The fantastic no-stick coating on the unit allowed me to wipe the egg off with one swipe of a towel. I was impressed.

Once I slowed down and used the machine like it was intended it was smooth sailing. The bread got properly toasted and the eggs cooked beautifully. My 12-year-old got the hang of using the sandwich maker on the first try.

I liked how the yolk stayed perfectly runny for those in our family that like runny yolks. For those that didn't like runny yolk, I simply scrambled the egg up with a fork a little bit after I dropped the egg in.

Timing is everything
What I didn't like is that there wasn't a reliable timer on the unit. It does have a preheat light, but as the manual says, this light doesn't indicate when the sandwich is done. Setting a kitchen timer to the suggested five minutes isn't a good remedy, either. We found that it can take anywhere from three to six minutes for a sandwich to cook, depending on the ingredients.

Eventually I found that it was best to just lift the lid up and take a peek every couple of minutes. This means you need to stick around and stay alert. It isn't an appliance you can set and leave to cook while you get ready for your day.

Don't smoosh

When using a panini maker, you may be used to squishing your sandwiches, but don't do that with a breakfast sandwich maker. Gently place the lid on top of your bread; it doesn't need to close completely to cook. If you do smoosh the lid down into place the egg with burst out of the appliance and will get all over your countertops.

Bread switch-up

All of the pictures on the box showed sandwiches made with round breads like bagels and English muffins, but we decided to give sliced loaf bread a try, too. You have to smash the edges of the bread into the unit just a bit, but it still came out perfectly toasted.

Cleaning up

Cleaning the breakfast sandwich maker is easy, too. Lifting the lid releases the sandwich making rings. They can be put in the dishwasher or can be washed by hand in hot, soapy water.

The plates on the unit can't be removed, but they can be wiped with a soapy sponge and then "rinsed" with a sponge damped with clean, warm water.

After you clean the unit, everything should be dried and coated with a non-stick cooking spray or wiped with vegetable oil to keep everything non-stick and tarnish-free.

CLASSIC BREAKFAST SANDWICH RECIPES

Creamy Brie Pancake Sandwich

Servings: 1
Cooking Time: 5 Minutes

Ingredients:
- 2 frozen pancakes
- 1 tablespoon raspberry jam
- 1 ounce Brie, chopped
- 1 large egg

Directions:
1. Preheat the breakfast sandwich maker.
2. Place one of the pancakes inside the bottom tray of the sandwich maker and spread the raspberry jam on top.
3. Sprinkle the chopped brie on top of the pancake.
4. Slide the egg tray into place and crack the egg into it.
5. Top the egg with the other pancake.
6. Close the sandwich maker and cook for 4 to 5 minutes until the egg is cooked through.
7. Carefully rotate the egg tray out of the sandwich maker then open the sandwich maker and enjoy your sandwich.

Hot Pork Sausage And Srambled Egg Sandwich

Servings: 1
Cooking Time: 4 Minutes

Ingredients:
- 2 ounces ground Pork Sausage, cooked
- 1 ounce shredded Cheddar Cheese
- 1 Egg
- ¼ tsp dried Thyme
- 1 Biscuit
- ½ tsp Hot Pepper Sauce
- Salt and Pepper, to taste

Directions:
1. Preheat and grease the sandwich maker with cooking spray.
2. Cut the biscuit in half and place one half inside the bottom ring.
3. Top with the sausage and cheddar, and sprinkle the hot sauce over.
4. Lower the top ring and cooking plate, and crack the egg into it.
5. Season with salt and pepper and sprinkle the thyme over.
6. Close the unit and wait 4 minutes before rotating clockwise to open.
7. Serve and enjoy!

Nutrition:
- Info
- Calories 455 Total Fats 33g Carbs 13g Protein 26g Fiber 0.4g

Chocolate Hazelnut French Toast Panini

Servings: 4
Cooking Time: 6 Minutes

Ingredients:

- 6 large eggs
- 1 cup whole milk
- 1/2 cup heavy cream
- 1/4 cup fresh orange juice (from about 1 medium orange)
- 2 tablespoons vanilla extract
- 2 tablespoons cognac (optional)
- 2 tablespoons granulated sugar
- 1/2 teaspoon ground cinnamon
- Pinch of freshly grated nutmeg
- Salt
- 8 slices Texas toast or other thick white bread
- ½ cup hazelnut spread with cocoa
- ¼ cup chopped hazelnuts, toasted
- Confectioners' sugar, for garnish
- Pure maple syrup, for garnish

Directions:

1. Spread the hazelnut spread on 4 of the pieces of bread and then place the hazelnuts on top. Top with the pieces of bread.
2. Use a whisk to combine the eggs, milk, cream, orange juice, cognac, sugar, cinnamon, and vanilla. Put the sandwiches in a shallow baking dishes and cover with the mixture you just created. Allow the sandwiches to rest in the mixture for 10 minutes
3. Preheat your flip sandwich maker on medium high heat.
4. Cook the Panini for 6 to 7 minutes in your preheated flap sandwiched maker, flipping halfway through.
5. Top with confectioners' sugar and maple syrup

Mediterranean Sandwich

Servings: 4

Cooking Time: 20minutes

Ingredients:

- 4 rolls, ciabatta, split
- 4 oz. Feta cheese, crumbled
- 24 oz. spaghetti or marinara sauce, divided
- 7 ½ oz. artichoke hearts, marinated, quartered and then chopped
- 2 Tomatoes, sliced
- 1 lb. Deli Turkey sliced thinly

Directions:

1. Spread 2 tbsp. marinara sauce on 4 roll halves.
2. Top the halves with cheese, turkey, tomato artichokes and again cheese. Spread 2 tbsp. Sauce and place the turkey. Top with the second roll hales.
3. Cook on the sandwich maker for 5 minutes.
4. Serve and enjoy!

Pork Sandwiches

Servings: 10
Cooking Time: 6 Hours

Ingredients:
- 1 Onion, sliced
- ¾ cup Chicken broth, reduced-sodium
- 1 cup Parsley, minutesced
- 7 cloves of garlic, minutesced
- 2 tbsp. Cider Vinegar
- 1 tbsp. lemon juice + 1 ½ tsp.
- 2 tsp. Cuminutes, ground
- 1 tsp. Mustard, ground
- 1 tsp. oregano, dried
- ½ tsp. of Salt
- ½ tsp. Black pepper
- 1 (4 lb.) Pork shoulder, boneless
- 1 ¼ cups Mayo, fat-free
- 2 tbsp. Dijon mustard
- 10 Hamburger buns
- 1 ¼ cups of shredded Swiss cheese
- 1 Onion, sliced into rings
- 2 dill pickles, whole, sliced

Directions:
1. Prepare the pork the night before. Place the broth and onion in a slow cooker. In a bowl combine black pepper, salt, oregano, mustard, cuminutes, lemon juice, vinegar, 5 cloves of garlic and parsley. Stir well and rub the pork. Add in the cooker and cook 6-8 hours.
2. Remove the meat and let it rest for about 10 minutes before you slice it.
3. In a bowl combine the remaining lemon and garlic, mustard and mayo. Spread over the buns (split the buns). Layer the bottom buns with pickles, onions, cheese, and pork. Top with half-bun.
4. Cook on a sandwich maker for about 3 minutes.
5. Serve and enjoy!

Prosciutto And Pesto Panini

Servings: 4
Cooking Time: 8 Minutes

Ingredients:

- One 10-ounce loaf Ciabatta, halved horizontally and soft interior removed
- 1/3 cup Pesto
- Extra-virgin olive oil
- 1/3 pound Prosciutto de Parma, thinly sliced
- Tapenade (optional)
- 1/4 pound Fontina cheese, thinly sliced
- 1/2 cup baby arugula or basil, optional
- Coarse salt and fresh ground pepper

Directions:

1. Spread pesto on one of the interior sides and olive oil on the other.
2. Put in a layer of prosciutto, then arugula or basil, then cheese. Top it off with a light drizzle of olive oil and a sprinkle of salt and pepper. Top with the other piece of bread.
3. Brush the inside each piece of bread with the dressing. Then top the bottom pieces of bread with cheese. Add the mortadella, salami, tomatoes and pepperoncini's
4. Cook the Panini on medium-high heat for 8 minutes, flipping halfway through. The bread should be brown, and the cheese should be melted.

Ultimate Blt Melt

Servings: 1
Cooking Time: 8 Minutes

Ingredients:
- 1 multigrain English muffin, split
- 1 Tbsp. mayonnaise
- 1 slice tomato
- 2 slices smoked bacon
- ½ slice cheddar cheese
- ½ slice Monterey Jack cheese
- Baby spinach leaves
- 1 Tbsp. milk
- 1 egg
- 1 Tbsp. diced onion
- 1 tsp. diced jalapeño
- Sea salt and pepper

Directions:
1. Spread mayonnaise on both English muffin halves. Place one half into the bottom ring of breakfast sandwich maker, mayo side up. Place tomato, bacon, cheddar cheese, Monterey Jack cheese and spinach leaves on top.
2. In a small bowl, whisk together milk, egg, onion, jalapeño, sea salt and pepper. Lower the cooking plate and top ring; pour in egg mixture. Top with other muffin half.
3. Close the cover and cook for 4 to 5 minutes or until egg is cooked through and cheeses are melted. Gently slide the egg plate out and remove sandwich with a rubber spatula.

Gruyere, Apple And Ham Sandwich

Servings: 1
Cooking Time: 5 Minutes

Ingredients:
- 1 Ciabatta roll, sliced in half
- 1 slice ham
- A few apple slices
- 1 slice gruyere cheese
- 1 Tbsp. milk
- 2 tsp. diced onion
- 1 egg
- Sea salt and pepper

Directions:
1. Place one Ciabatta roll half into the bottom ring of breakfast sandwich maker. Place ham, apple slices and gruyere cheese on top.
2. In a small bowl whisk together milk, onion, egg, sea salt and pepper. Lower the cooking plate and top ring; pour egg mixture into egg plate. Top with other roll half.
3. Close the cover and cook for 4 to 5 minutes or until egg is cooked and cheese is melted. Remove sandwich with a rubber spatula.

Classic Egg, Ham And Cheese

Servings: 1
Cooking Time: 5 Minutes

Ingredients:

- 1 toasted English muffin, sliced
- 2 slices deli ham
- 1 slice cheddar cheese
- 1 large egg

Directions:

1. Preheat the breakfast sandwich maker.
2. Place half of the English muffin, cut-side up, inside the bottom tray of the sandwich maker.
3. Fold the slices of ham on top of the English muffin half and top with the slice of cheddar cheese.
4. Slide the egg tray into place and crack the egg into it.
5. Top the egg with the other half of the English muffin.
6. Close the sandwich maker and cook for 4 to 5 minutes until the egg is cooked through.
7. Carefully rotate the egg tray out of the sandwich maker then open the sandwich maker and enjoy your sandwich.

Croissant Sandwich With Sausage, Egg, And Cheddar

Servings: 1
Cooking Time: 5 Minutes

Ingredients:

- 5 Slices of Cooked Sausage
- 1 Egg
- 1 slice Cheddar
- 1 Croissant
- 2 tsp Mayonnaise
- Salt and Pepper, to taste

Directions:

1. Preheat and grease the sandwich maker.
2. Cut the croissant in half and spread the mayonnaise over the cut-side of each half.
3. Place one half of the croissant with the cut-side up in the bottom ring.
4. Top with the cheddar and sausage.
5. Lower the cooking plate and crack the egg into it. Season with salt and pepper.
6. Top with the second croissant half, placing it with the cut-side down.
7. Close the unit and cook for 4 to 5 minutes.
8. Rotate clockwise carefully, and transfer to a plate.
9. Serve and enjoy!

Nutrition:

- Info
- Calories 580 Total Fats 41.5g Carbs 27g Protein 24g Fiber 1.5g

Classic Grilled Cheese Sandwich

Servings: 1
Cooking Time: 4 Minutes

Ingredients:
- 2 slices of Bread
- 1 ounce shredded Mozzarella
- 1 ounce shredded Gouda
- 2 tsp Butter

Directions:
1. Preheat the Hamilton Beach Breakfast Sandwich and grease it with some cooking spray.
2. Cut the bread slices so that they can fit inside the sandwich maker.
3. Spread 1 tsp of butter onto each of the slices.
4. Place one slice of the bread into the bottom ring with the butter-side down.
5. Top with the cheeses.
6. Lower the top ring and add the second slice, placing it with the butter-side up.
7. Close the appliance and cook for about 4 minutes, or less if you want it less crispy.
8. Slide out by rotating clockwise. Lift the cover carefully and transfer the sandwich to a plate.
9. Serve and enjoy!

Nutrition:
- Info
- Calories 453 Total Fats 25g Carbs 39g Protein 21g Fiber 6g

Buffalo Patty Melt Panini

Servings: 4
Cooking Time: 4 Minutes

Ingredients:
- 2 tablespoons unsalted butter
- 1 large Vidalia or other sweet onion, sliced
- 1 pound lean ground beef
- 1 tablespoon Worcestershire sauce
- 1/2 teaspoon garlic powder
- 1/4 teaspoon black pepper
- 8 slices seedless rye
- 1/4 pound thinly sliced Swiss cheese, about 8 slices
- 1/4 cup blue cheese dressing
- 1 cup mayonnaise
- 1 cup buffalo hot sauce

Directions:
1. Melt the butter in a large skillet on medium heat. Add the onions and cook for about 20 minutes. While the onions are cooking combine the beef, Worcestershire sauce, and the seasoning. Form the beef into patties that are similar in shape to the bread. Place the patties in the skillet with the onions for the last 5 minutes of cooking. Flip the meat once halfway through.
2. Mix the buffalo sauce and mayonnaise in a medium bowl.
3. Spread the buffalo sauce mixture on one side of each piece of bread.
4. Put a slice of cheese on a piece of bread then a patty, the onions and top with another slice of cheese and top with another piece of bread. Repeat the process with the remaining sandwiches.
5. Cook the sandwiches for 4 minutes on medium heat, and make sure to flip halfway through. The bread should be brown, and the cheese should be melted. Serve the sandwiches with a side of the blue cheese dressing.

Olive And Cheese Snack

Servings: 1
Cooking Time: 3 Minutes

Ingredients:
- 1 Bread Slice
- 1 ounce Shredded Cheese
- 1 Basil Leaf, chopped
- 2 Kalamata Olives, diced

Directions:
1. Grease the unit and preheat it until the green light appears.
2. Cut the bread slice so that it can fit inside the unit, and place it on top of the bottom ring.
3. Top with the olives, basil, and cheese.
4. Close the lid and cook for 3 minutes.
5. Rotate clockwise and open carefully.
6. Transfer with a non-metal spatula and enjoy!

Nutrition:
- Info
- Calories 205 Total Fats 12.7g Carbs 15g Protein 10g Fiber 2.1g

Peanut Butter Waffle With Banana

Servings: 1
Cooking Time: 4 Minutes

Ingredients:
- 1 Frozen Waffle
- 1 tbsp Peanut Butter
- ¼ Banana, sliced

Directions:
1. Preheat the sandwich maker and grease it with some cooking spray.
2. Place the waffle on top of the bottom ring.
3. Spread the peanut butter over and close the lid.
4. Cook for about 3 minutes.
5. Open carefully and transfer to a plate.
6. Top with the banana slices and enjoy!

Nutrition:
- Info
- Calories 214 Total Fats 11g Carbs 25g Protein 6.3g Fiber 2.9g

Maple Bacon Waffle Sandwich

Servings: 1
Cooking Time: 4 Minutes

Ingredients:
- 2 small round waffles (store bought or homemade)
- Maple syrup
- 2 strips maple bacon
- 1 slice cheddar cheese
- 1 egg
- 1 Tbsp. milk
- Sea salt and pepper

Directions:
1. Place one waffle in the bottom of sandwich maker. Drizzle some maple syrup on top, then the maple bacon and cheddar cheese.
2. Lower the cooking plate and top ring. In a small bowl, whisk together egg, milk, sea salt and pepper; pour into egg plate. Top with other waffle.
3. Close the cover and cook for 4 to 5 minutes or until egg is cooked through and cheese is melted. Slide the egg plate out and remove sandwich with a rubber spatula. Cut in half.

Red Pepper And Goat Cheese Sandwich

Servings: 1
Cooking Time: 5 Minutes

Ingredients:

- 2 slices multigrain bread
- 1 ounce goat cheese
- 2 slices fresh red pepper
- 1 slice red onion
- Salt and pepper to taste
- 1 large egg

Directions:

1. Preheat the breakfast sandwich maker.
2. Place one slice of bread inside the bottom tray of the sandwich maker.
3. Top the bread with the goat cheese, red pepper and red onion. Season with salt and pepper to taste.
4. Slide the egg tray into place and crack the egg into it. Use a fork to stir the egg, just breaking the yolk.
5. Place the second slice of bread on top of the egg.
6. Close the sandwich maker and cook for 4 to 5 minutes until the egg is cooked through.
7. Carefully rotate the egg tray out of the sandwich maker then open the sandwich maker to enjoy your sandwich.

Almond Flour Waffle And Sausage Sandwich

Servings: 1

Cooking Time: 4 Minutes

Ingredients:
- 2 Almond Flour Waffles
- 1 Frozen Sausage Pattie
- 1 slice American Cheese
- 2 Red Onion Rings
- 2 Tomato Slices

Directions:
1. Preheat the sandwich maker until the green light appears and grease the unit with cooking spray.
2. Add one waffle to the bottom ring and top with the sausage pattie.
3. Add the tomato slices and red onion over, and place the cheese on top.
4. Lower the top ring and add the second waffle.
5. Close the unit and cook for 4 minutes.
6. Rotate clockwise and open.
7. Serve and enjoy!

Nutrition:
- Info
- Calories 345 Total Fats 28g Carbs 14g Protein 20g Fiber 7g

The Thanksgiving Turkey Cuban Panini

Servings: 4
Cooking Time: 7 Minutes

Ingredients:
- 2 tablespoons mayonnaise
- 2 tablespoons Dijon mustard
- 2 tablespoons leftover cranberry sauce
- Salt and freshly ground black pepper
- 4 slices good quality Italian bread
- 4 slices Swiss cheese
- 2 slices cooked ham
- 6 slices leftover cooked turkey
- 8 dill pickle slices
- Olive oil

Directions:
1. Mix together the first mayonnaise, cranberry sauce, and Dijon mustard using a whisk. Salt and pepper to taste. Combine the mixture with the cabbage until well coated.
2. Spread a layer of the newly made cranberry Dijon sauce on what's going to be the inside of 2 pieces of bread. Put a layer of cheese, then turkey, a layer of the ham, a layer of pickles, and another layer of cheese on the pieces of bread. Top with another piece of bread. Brush the top and bottom of the sandwich with olive oil
3. Cook the sandwiches for 6 to 7 minutes on medium high heat, and make sure to flip halfway through. The bread should be toasted, and the cheese should be melted. Once you're ready to serve, slice the sandwiches in half.

Chocolate Croissant

Servings: 1
Cooking Time: 3 Minutes

Ingredients:
- 2 ounces Chocolate, chopped
- 1 Croissant
- 1 tsp Heavy Cream

Directions:
1. Preheat the sandwich maker and grease it with some cooking spray.
2. Cut the croissant in half and place one half on top of the bottom ring, with the cut-side up.
3. Arrange the chocolate pieces on top and sprinkle with the heavy cream.
4. Lower the top ring and add the second croissant part, with the cut-side down.
5. Cook for 3 minutes.
6. Open carefully and transfer to a plate.
7. Serve and enjoy!

Nutrition:
- Info
- Calories 283 Total Fats 14g Carbs 32g Protein 6g Fiber 1.8g

Crunchy Nutella And Strawberry Bagel

Servings: 1
Cooking Time: 3 Minutes

Ingredients:

- ½ Bagel
- 1 tbsp Nutella
- 4 Strawberries, sliced
- 1 tsp chopped Hazelnuts

Directions:

1. Preheat the Hamilton Beach Breakfast Sandwich Maker until the green light appears. Spray with some cooking spray.
2. Spread the Nutella over the bagel.
3. Place the bagel on top of the bottom ring, with the cut-side up.
4. Arrange the strawberry slices over, and sprinkle with the hazelnuts.
5. Close the lid and cook for 3 minutes.
6. Rotate the handle clockwise to open.
7. Serve and enjoy!

Nutrition:

- Info
- Calories 220 Total Fats 8g Carbs 32g Protein 5.8g Fiber 2.2g

Mexican-style Egg And Beans Sandwich

Servings: 1

Cooking Time: 5 Minutes

Ingredients:

- 2 slices whole wheat bread
- 1 ounce shredded Mexican cheese
- 2 tbsp. refried beans
- 1 large egg
- 1 tbsp. sliced green onion

Directions:

1. Preheat the breakfast sandwich maker.
2. Place one slice of bread inside the bottom tray of the sandwich maker.
3. Top the bread with the refried beans and cheese.
4. Slide the egg tray into place and crack the egg into it. Use a fork to stir the egg, just breaking the yolk.
5. Sprinkle the green onion over the egg then place the second piece of bread on top of the egg.
6. Close the sandwich maker and cook for 4 to 5 minutes until the egg is cooked through.
7. Carefully rotate the egg tray out of the sandwich maker then open the sandwich maker to enjoy your sandwich.

Sausage & Gravy Biscuit

Servings: 1
Cooking Time: 4 Minutes

Ingredients:

- 1 store bought or homemade biscuit, sliced in half
- 1 – 2 Tbsp. store bought country gravy
- 1 precooked sausage patty
- 1 slice cheddar cheese
- 1 egg

Directions:

1. Spread the country gravy on both biscuit halves. Place one biscuit half, cut side up into the bottom ring of breakfast sandwich maker. Place sausage patty and cheddar cheese on top.
2. Lower the cooking plate and top ring; crack an egg into the egg plate and pierce to break the yolk. Top with other biscuit half.
3. Close the cover and cook for 4 to 5 minutes or until egg is cooked through. Gently slide the egg plate out and remove sandwich with a rubber spatula.

Ham And Relish Melt

Servings: 1
Cooking Time: 5 Minutes

Ingredients:

- 2 slices white or multigrain bread
- Butter
- 1 Tbsp. sweet pickle relish
- 1 slice ham
- 1 slice cheddar cheese
- 1 egg
- Sea salt and pepper

Directions:

1. Butter the outside of each slice of bread. Spread relish on the inside of each slice. Place one slice into the bottom ring of breakfast sandwich maker, relish side up. Place ham and cheddar cheese on top.
2. Lower the cooking plate and top ring; crack an egg into the egg plate and pierce to break the yolk. Season with sea salt and pepper. Top with other slice of bread.
3. Close the cover and cook for 4 to 5 minutes or until egg is cooked and cheese is melted. Carefully remove sandwich with a rubber spatula.

Ground Turkey Taco Cups

Servings: 1
Cooking Time: 5 Minutes

Ingredients:
- 1 Flour Tortilla
- 1 ounce shredded Cheddar
- 1 tsp Sour Cream
- 1 tsp Salsa
- 2 ounces cooked Ground Chicken
- 2 tsp chopped Onion
- 1 tsp chopped Parsley

Directions:
1. Preheat and grease the sandwich maker.
2. Slide out the cooking plate – you will not need it for this recipe.
3. Place the tortilla into the ring, tucking it, so that it looks like a cup.
4. In a small bowl, combine the rest of the ingredients.
5. Fill the taco cup with the chicken filling.
6. Close the lid and cook for 5 minutes.
7. Rotate clockwise and lift to open, then transfer to a plate.
8. Serve and enjoy!

Nutrition:
- Info
- Calories 305 Total Fats 14.5g Carbs 19.6g Protein 23.2g Fiber 1.3g

Sour Cream And Crab Cake Sandwich

Servings: 1

Cooking Time: 3 ½ Minutes

Ingredients:

- 1 frozen Crab Cake Pattie
- 2 tsp Sour Cream
- 1 slice American Cheese
- ½ Pickle, sliced
- 1 Biscuit

Directions:

1. Preheat the sandwich maker and grease it with some cooking spray.
2. Cut the biscuit in half and place one half to the bottom ring of the unit.
3. Spread half of the sour cream over and add the crab cake on top.
4. Spread the remaining sour cream over the crab cake, arrange the pickle slices over, and top with the cheese.
5. Lower the top ring and add the second biscuit half.
6. Close the unit and cook for 3 ½ minutes.
7. Open carefully and transfer to a plate.
8. Serve and enjoy!

Nutrition:

- Info
- Calories 340 Total Fats 26g Carbs 21g Protein 23g Fiber 3g

Eggs Benedict With Ham

Servings: 1
Cooking Time: 5 Minutes

Ingredients:

- 4 tablespoons unsalted butter
- 1 large egg yolk
- 2 teaspoons lemon juice
- Pinch cayenne pepper
- Pinch salt
- 1 whole wheat bagel, sliced
- ½ cup fresh spinach leaves
- 2 slices cooked bacon
- 1 large egg, beaten

Directions:

1. Preheat the breakfast sandwich maker.
2. Melt the butter in a small saucepan over medium heat.
3. Blend the egg yolks, lemon juice, cayenne and salt in a blender then drizzle into the saucepan.
4. Cook for 10 seconds, stirring well, then remove from heat and set aside.
5. Place half of the bagel, cut-side up, inside the bottom tray of the sandwich maker.
6. Top the bagel half with spinach leaves. Break the bacon slices in half and place them on top of the spinach.
7. Slide the egg tray into place and pour the beaten egg into it.
8. Top the egg with the other half of the bagel.
9. Close the sandwich maker and cook for 4 to 5 minutes until the egg is cooked through.
10. Carefully rotate the egg tray out of the sandwich maker then open the sandwich maker.
11. Take the top bagel off the sandwich and drizzle the eggs with the hollandaise sauce.
12. Replace the bagel half and enjoy your sandwich.

Prosciutto And Egg Bagel Panini

Servings: 2
Cooking Time: 3 Minutes

Ingredients:

- 2 eggs
- 2 everything bagels (or any favorite bagel)
- 2 tablespoons mayonnaise
- 2 slices American cheese
- 4 slices prosciutto
- 2 handfuls baby arugula
- Kosher salt
- Ground black pepper
- Olive oil
- 2 teaspoon butter

Directions:

1. Use a whisk to beat the egg with a pinch of salt and pepper.   Place the butter in a skillet and melt it on medium heat. Use a spoon to stir the eggs and push them across the pan. Cook until the eggs set, about 1 to 20 minutes.
2. Cut the bagels in half horizontally. Spread the mayonnaise on the inside of the bagel. Layer the eggs, on the inside of 2 of the bagel halves, then the cheese, then the arugula, then the prosciutto. Top with the remaining pieces of bagel. Brush the top and bottom of the sandwiches with olive oil.
3. Cook the Panini on medium heat for 2 to 3 minutes, flipping halfway through. The bagels should be toasted, and the cheese should be melted.

Taleggio And Salami Panini With Spicy Fennel Honey

Servings: 6
Cooking Time: 10 Minutes

Ingredients:
- 1/3 cup honey
- 1 tablespoon fennel seeds
- 2 teaspoons chili flakes
- 1/2 loaf focaccia, cut into 4-inch squares
- 1 pound Taleggio, rind washed, room temperature, thinly sliced
- 12 slices fennel salami, thinly sliced

Directions:
1. Put the chili, fennel, and honey in a small saucepan and heat on medium heat. Allow the mixture to cook for 3 to 5 minutes.
2. Cut the focaccia in half horizontally. Layer the cheese on one piece of bread and layer the salami on top. Top the salami with a nice drizzle of the honey. Put the other piece of bread on top.
3. Brush the inside each piece of bread with the dressing. Then top the bottom pieces of bread with cheese. Add the mortadella, salami, tomatoes and pepperoncini's
4. Cook the Panini on medium-high heat for 10 minutes, flipping halfway through. The bread should be brown, and the cheese should be melted.
5. Top with more honey and serve warm.

Buffalo Chicken Panini

Servings: 4
Cooking Time: 4 Minutes

Ingredients:
- 2 cups shredded cooked chicken
- 1 large sweet onion, sliced
- 8 slices seedless rye
- 1/4 pound thinly sliced Swiss cheese, about 8 slices
- 1/4 cup blue cheese dressing
- 1 cup mayonnaise
- 1 cup buffalo hot sauce
- 2 tablespoons unsalted butter
- blue cheese dressing

Directions:
1. Melt the butter in a large skillet on medium heat. Add the onions and cook for about 20 minutes.
2. Mix the buffalo sauce and mayonnaise in a medium bowl and toss with the chicken.
3. Put a slice of cheese on a piece of bread then the chicken, the onions and top with another slice of cheese and top with another piece of bread. Repeat the process with the remaining sandwiches. Spread the butter on the top and bottom of the sandwich
4. Cook the sandwiches for 4 minutes on medium heat, and make sure to flip halfway through. The bread should be brown, and the cheese should be melted. Serve the sandwiches with a side of the blue cheese dressing.

Bacon Egg And Sausage Breakfast Panini

Servings: 2
Cooking Time: 6 Minutes

Ingredients:

- 2 pita breads
- 1/2cup pesto
- 2 eggs
- 1 cup shredded sharp cheddar cheese
- 1 cup shredded Monterey Jack cheese
- 1 cup shredded mozzarella cheese
- 1 pork sausage patty, cooked
- 2 strips bacon, cooked
- 1/3 cup roasted red pepper
- 1-2 tablespoons butter, melted
- 2 scallions, chopped

Directions:

1. Use a whisk to beat the egg with a pinch of salt and pepper. Place the butter in a skillet and melt it on medium heat. Use a spoon to stir the eggs and push them across the pan. Cook until the eggs set, about 1 to 2 minutes.
2. Chop the sausage into small pieces. Spread the pesto on half of both pieces of pita. Top the pitas with half the cheese, then eggs, bacon, sausage, bell pepper, the remaining, cheese and then top with the scallions. Fold the other side of the pita on top of the filling, and spread the butter on the outside of the pitas.
3. Cook the Panini on medium heat for 4 to 6 minutes, flipping halfway through. The bread should be brown, and the cheese should be melted.

The Ham & Cheese

Servings: 1
Cooking Time: 4 Minutes

Ingredients:
- 1 English muffin, split
- Grainy mustard
- 1 slice honey spiral ham
- 1 slice cheddar cheese
- 1 egg
- Red Hot sauce

Directions:
1. Spread some grainy mustard on both halves of English muffin. Place one half, mustard side up into the bottom ring of breakfast sandwich maker. Place ham and cheddar cheese on top.
2. Lower the cooking plate and top ring; crack an egg into the egg plate and pierce to break the yolk. Sprinkle a few drops of Red Hot sauce on the egg and top with other muffin half.
3. Close the cover and cook for 4 to 5 minutes or until egg is cooked through. Gently slide the egg plate out and remove sandwich with a rubber spatula.

Lemony Delicious Summer Vegetable Panini

Servings: 4

Cooking Time: 4 Minutes

Ingredients:
- 1 tablespoons olive oil
- 1 small onion, sliced
- 1 medium yellow squash, thinly sliced
- 1 medium zucchini, thinly sliced
- 1 red bell pepper, sliced
- 2 teaspoons + lemon zest
- ¼ teaspoon salt
- 4 Ciabatta rolls or 4 pieces of focaccia
- 1/8 teaspoon ground black pepper
- 1 cup part-skim ricotta cheese
- 2 teaspoons lemon zest
- 1 ½ teaspoons lemon juice
- 1/8 teaspoon salt
- 1/8 teaspoon ground black pepper

Directions:
1. Place the oil in a skillet and heat it on medium high heat. Cook the onions in the oil for about 3 to 4 seconds, until they start to soften. Mix in the squash, peppers and zucchini and cook for another 5 to 7 minutes. Mix in the first 2 teaspoons of lemon zest and 1/8 teaspoon of pepper and the ¼ teaspoon of salt. Remove the mixture from the heat and set aside in a bowl.

2. Mix the last 5Ingredients:in a bowl.

3. Slice the rolls in half horizontally and place a layer of the ricotta mixture on the inside of each piece of bread.

4. Place the vegetable mixture on the bottom pieces of bread. Pot the top pieces of bread on the vegetables, making sure the ricotta side is touching the vegetables.

5. Cook the Panini on medium high heat for 3 to 4 minutes, flipping halfway through. The bread should be brown, and the cheese should be melted.

Avocado Sandwich With Egg, Ham And Cheese

Servings: 1

Cooking Time: 4 Minutes

Ingredients:

- 4 Large Avocado Slices
- 1 Egg
- 1 Ham Slice
- 1 slice American Cheese
- Salt and Pepper, to taste

Directions:

1. Preheat the sandwich maker until the green light appears and grease it with cooking spray.
2. Arrange two of the avocado slices on the bottom ring.
3. Place the ham and cheese on top.
4. Lower the cooking plate and crack the egg into it. Season with salt and pepper.
5. Top with the remaining avocado slices.
6. Close the sandwich maker and cook for 4 minutes.
7. Side out and rotate clockwise. Open and transfer the sandwich with a spatula, very carefully, as you are using avocado slices, not bread.
8. Serve and enjoy!

Nutrition:

- Info
- Calories 580 Total Fats 44g Carbs 21g Protein 28g Fiber 12g

Chipotle Chicken Sandwich

Servings: 1
Cooking Time: 5 Minutes

Ingredients:
- 1 ciabatta roll, sliced
- 1 cooked chicken patty
- 1 slice Pepper Jack cheese
- 1 tbsp. chipotle mayonnaise
- 1 large egg
- 1 slice red onion
- 1 piece romaine lettuce, torn in half

Directions:
1. Preheat the breakfast sandwich maker.
2. Place half of the ciabatta roll, cut-side up, inside the bottom tray of the sandwich maker.
3. Top the ciabatta with the chicken patty and Pepper Jack cheese.
4. Slide the egg tray into place and crack the egg into it. Use a fork to stir the egg, just breaking the yolk.
5. Brush the other half of the ciabatta roll with the chipotle mayonnaise.
6. Place the second half of the ciabatta on top of the egg.
7. Close the sandwich maker and cook for 4 to 5 minutes until the egg is cooked through.
8. Carefully rotate the egg tray out of the sandwich maker then open the sandwich maker.
9. Remove the top ciabatta roll and top the sandwich with the onion and lettuce. Replace the roll to enjoy the sandwich.

Bacon Mozzarella, Zucchini And Tomato Panini

Servings: 4

Cooking Time: 8 Minutes

Ingredients:

- 6 slices bacon
- 1/2 large zucchini, cut lengthwise into 1/4" slices and grilled
- 3 tbsp. extra-virgin olive oil, divided
- kosher salt
- Freshly ground black pepper
- 1 medium yellow tomato, thinly sliced
- 1 medium red tomato, thinly sliced
- 1 loaf Ciabatta, halved lengthwise
- 8 oz. mozzarella, thinly sliced
- 2 tbsp. Freshly Chopped Basil

Directions:

1. Put the tomatoes on a plate lined with paper towel in order to soak up any excess liquid.
2. Use a brush to coat the inside of the bread with olive oil. Put down a layer of zucchini, then bacon, basil, and finally tomatoes. Salt and pepper to taste and top with top piece of bread. Use a brush to coat the top and bottom of sandwich.
3. Spread the butter on one side of each piece of bread. Place 2 pieces of bacon on the unbuttered side of a piece of bread, then 2 tomatoes and a ¼ of the cheese. Then top with the another piece of bread making sure the butter side is on top.
4. Cook the Panini on medium high heat for 6 to 8 minutes, flipping halfway through. The bread should be brown, and the cheese should be melted.

Peanut Butter Bagel Sandwich

Servings: 4
Cooking Time: 5minutes

Ingredients:
- 4 Bagels, split
- ½ cup Marshmallows, minutesi
- ¼ cup chunks milk Chocolate
- ¼ cup Peanut butter, creamy
- 4 tbsp. unsalted Butter

Directions:
1. Preheat the sandwich maker on medium heat.
2. On one half spread the peanut butter evenly. Top with marshmallows and chocolate chunks. Top with the other half of the beagles.
3. Butter the sandwich maker and add the sandwiches. Press and cook for 5 minutesutes, or until the marshmallows and chocolate melt.
4. Let it cool for about 10 minutes.
5. Serve and enjoy!

Spinach, Parmesan And Egg White

Servings: 1

Cooking Time: 5 Minutes

Ingredients:

- 1 toasted English muffin, sliced
- ½ cup baby spinach leaves
- 2 large egg whites
- 1 tablespoon grated parmesan cheese
- 1 clove garlic, minced

Directions:

1. Preheat the breakfast sandwich maker.
2. Place half of the English muffin, cut-side up, inside the bottom tray of the sandwich maker.
3. Arrange the baby spinach leaves on top of the English muffin.
4. Beat the egg whites, parmesan cheese and garlic in a small bowl.
5. Slide the egg tray into place and pour the egg mixture into it.
6. Top the egg with the other half of the English muffin.
7. Close the sandwich maker and cook for 4 to 5 minutes until the egg is cooked through.
8. Carefully rotate the egg tray out of the sandwich maker then open the sandwich maker and enjoy your sandwich.

Pressed Turkey Sandwich

Servings: 1
Cooking Time: 10minutes

Ingredients:

- 2 slices of bread, whole grain
- 2 tsp. Mustard
- 1/8 tsp. Rosemary, dried or fresh ¼ tsp.
- 1 grated Minutesi Cheese Round
- 2 oz. Turkey breast, smoked
- 4-5 slices of ripe pear
- Baby Spinach, a handful

Directions:

1. Preheat the Panini press.
2. Mix the mustard with the rosemary.
3. Spread the mustard on the bread slices and top one slice with turkey, ½ cheese, spinach and add the remaining cheese.
4. Put the second bread slice on top and grill on the Panini press until the cheese melts and the bread becomes golden.
5. Let it rest for 1 minutes and then serve.

Choco-coconut Nut Quesadilla

Servings: 1
Cooking Time: 3 Minutes

Ingredients:
- 2 small corn tortillas
- 2 tsp. chocolate hazelnut spread
- 2 tsp. almond butter
- Shredded coconut
- Honey or agave nectar
- Cinnamon

Directions:
1. Spread chocolate hazelnut spread and almond butter on both tortillas. Place one tortilla into the bottom ring of breakfast sandwich maker, nut butter side up. Sprinkle with coconut, drizzle with honey or agave and add a dash of cinnamon. Cover with other tortilla
2. Close the cover and cook for 3 to 4 minutes or until warmed through. Gently remove with a rubber spatula. Slice in half or roll up.

Smoked Salmon And Brie Sandwich

Servings: 1
Cooking Time: 5 Minutes

Ingredients:

- 1 whole wheat English muffin, sliced
- 2 ounces smoked salmon
- 1 ounce Brie cheese, chopped
- 1 tbsp. chopped chives
- ½ tsp. chopped capers
- 1 large egg

Directions:

1. Preheat the breakfast sandwich maker.
2. Place half of the English muffin, cut-side up, inside the bottom tray of the sandwich maker.
3. Top the muffin with the salmon, chopped brie, chives and capers.
4. Slide the egg tray into place and crack the egg into it. Use a fork to stir the egg, just breaking the yolk.
5. Place the second half of the English muffin on top of the egg. Close the sandwich maker and cook for 4 to 5 minutes until the egg is cooked through
6. .Carefully rotate the egg tray out of the sandwich maker then open the sandwich maker to enjoy your sandwich

The Ultimate Chicken, Spinach And Mozzarella Sandwich

Servings: 1
Cooking Time: 4 Minutes

Ingredients:
- 1 small Hamburger Bun
- 3 ounces cooked and chopped Chicken
- 1 tbsp Cream Cheese
- 1 ounce shredded Mozzarella
- 1 tbsp canned Corn
- 2 tbsp chopped Spinach

Directions:
1. Preheat and grease the sandwich maker.
2. Cut the bun in half and brush the cream cheese on the insides.
3. Add one half to the bottom ring, with the cut-side up.
4. Place the chicken on top and top with the spinach, corn, and mozzarella.
5. Lower the top ring and add the second half of the bun, the cut-side down.
6. Cook for 4 minutes.
7. Rotate clockwise and lift to open.
8. Serve and enjoy!

Nutrition:
- Info
- Calories 402 Total Fats 15.5g Carbs 32g Protein 32.5g Fiber 1.4g

Mixed Berry French Toast Panini

Servings: 4

Cooking Time: 6 Minutes

Ingredients:
- 6 large eggs
- 1 cup whole milk
- 1/2 cup heavy cream
- 1/4 cup fresh orange juice (from about 1 medium orange)
- 2 tablespoons vanilla extract
- 2 tablespoons cognac (optional)
- 2 tablespoons granulated sugar
- 1/2 teaspoon ground cinnamon
- Pinch of freshly grated nutmeg
- Salt
- 8 slices Texas toast or other thick white bread
- 1 cup blackberries
- 1 cup raspberries
- Confectioners' sugar, for garnish
- Pure maple syrup, for garnish

Directions:
1. Spread the cream cheese on what's going to be the inside of the pieces of bread and then place the strawberries on top of 4 of them. Top with the remaining pieces of bread.
2. Use a whisk to combine the eggs, milk, cream, orange juice, cognac, sugar, cinnamon, and vanilla. Put the sandwiches in a shallow baking dishes and cover with the mixture you just created. Allow sandwiches to rest in the mixture for 10 minutes.
3. Preheat your flip sandwich maker on medium high heat.
4. Cook the Panini for 6 to 7 minutes in your preheated flap sandwiched maker, flipping halfway through.
5. Top with confectioners' sugar and maple syrup.

Eggs Benedict Sandwich

Servings: 1
Cooking Time: 4 To 5 Minutes

Ingredients:
- 4 Baby Spinach Leaves
- 1 English Muffin
- 1 Slice Canadian Bacon
- 1 tbsp Hollandaise Sauce
- 1 Egg, lightly whisked

Directions:
1. Preheat the Hamilton Beach Breakfast Sandwich Maker and spray it with some cooking spray.
2. Split the muffin in half and add one half to the bottom ring.
3. Top with the baby spinach and bacon.
4. Lower the cooking plate and add the egg to it.
5. Top with the remaining muffin half and close the unit.
6. Let cook for 4 to 5 minutes.
7. Turn the handle clockwise and open carefully.
8. Transfer the sandwich with a plastic spatula to a plate.
9. Drizzle the Hollandaise Sauce on top.
10. Enjoy!

Nutrition:
- Info
- Calories 330 Total Fats 14.7g Carbs 31g Protein 19g Fiber 2.5g

Tomato, Egg And Avocado

Servings: 1
Cooking Time: 5 Minutes

Ingredients:

- 1 croissant, sliced
- 2 slices ripe tomato
- ¼ ripe avocado, pitted and sliced
- 1 slice Swiss cheese
- 1 large egg
- 1 tablespoon sliced green onion
- 2 teaspoons half-n-half

Directions:

1. Preheat the breakfast sandwich maker.
2. Place half of the croissant, cut-side up, inside the bottom tray of the sandwich maker.
3. Top the croissant with the tomato and avocado, then top with the slice of Swiss cheese.
4. Whisk together the egg, green onion and half-n-half in a small bowl.
5. Slide the egg tray into place and pour the egg mixture into it.
6. Top the egg with the other half of the croissant.
7. Close the sandwich maker and cook for 4 to 5 minutes until the egg is cooked through.
8. Carefully rotate the egg tray out of the sandwich maker then open the sandwich maker and enjoy your sandwich.

Turkey Salsa Melt

Servings: 1
Cooking Time: 4 Minutes

Ingredients:

- 2 ounces leftover Turkey, chopped up nicely
- 1 English Muffin
- 1 tbsp Salsa
- 1 ounce shredded Cheese by choice
- 1 tsp chopped Celery

Directions:

1. Preheat and grease the sandwich maker.
2. Cut the muffin in half and place one half on top of the bottom ring, with the cut-size up.
3. Combine the turkey and salsa and place on top of the muffin.
4. Add the celery on top and sprinkle the cheese over.
5. Lower the top ring and add the second half with he cut-size down.
6. Close and cook for 4 minutes.
7. Carefully open the lid and transfer to a plate.
8. Serve and enjoy!

Nutrition:

- Info
- Calories 410 Total Fats 22g Carbs 21g Protein 20g Fiber 0.9g

Spicy Sandwich

Servings: 1
Cooking Time: 5minutes

Ingredients:

- 1 Onion roll
- 1 tsp. Mayo
- 5 slices of Cooked Steak
- Shredded Cheese
- Salt and black pepper to taste
- Hot sauce to taste

Directions:

1. Slice the onion roll in two and spread the mayo and hot sauce.
2. Layer the cooked steak and add the cheese.
3. Season with black pepper and salt to taste. Cover with the other half of the roll.
4. Press on the sandwich maker for 5 minutes.
5. Serve and enjoy!

Apple Pie Sandwich

Servings: 4
Cooking Time: 5 Minutes

Ingredients:
- ½ cup of Mascarpone Cheese
- 2 tsp. Honey
- 4 tbsp. room temperature butter
- 8 slices of Cinnamon bread
- 1 apple, Granny Smith, cored and then sliced thinly
- 2 tbsp. Brown sugar, light

Directions:
1. In a bowl combine the honey and mascarpone. Whisk until fluffy and smooth.
2. Turn on medium-high heat and preheat the sandwich maker.
3. Spread butter on 2 bread slices. Flip them and spread 1 tbsp. of the mascarpone. Top with apple slices and close with the other bread slices.
4. Sprinkle with brown sugar.
5. Grill for 5 minutes.
6. Serve and enjoy!

Italian Egg Whites On Ciabatta

Servings: 1
Cooking Time: 5 Minutes

Ingredients:
- 1 ciabatta sandwich roll, sliced
- 1 teaspoon unsalted butter
- 1 slice mozzarella cheese
- 2 large egg whites
- 1 tablespoon skim milk
- 1 clove garlic, minced
- 1 teaspoon chopped chives
- 1/8 teaspoon dried Italian seasoning

Directions:
1. Preheat the breakfast sandwich maker.
2. Place half of ciabatta roll, cut-side up, inside the bottom tray of the sandwich maker.
3. Spread the butter on the ciabatta roll. Top with the slice of mozzarella cheese.
4. Whisk together the egg whites, milk, garlic, chives and Italian seasoning.
5. Slide the egg tray into place and pour the egg mixture into it.
6. Top the egg with the other half of the ciabatta roll.
7. Close the sandwich maker and cook for 4 to 5 minutes until the egg is cooked through.
8. Carefully rotate the egg tray out of the sandwich maker then open the sandwich maker and enjoy your sandwich.

Ham And Cheese Egg Biscuit Sandwich

Servings: 1

Cooking Time: 5 Minutes

Ingredients:

- 1 Biscuit, halved
- 2 Red Pepper Rings
- 1 Egg
- 1 Ham Slice
- 1 slice American Cheese
- Salt and Pepper, to taste

Directions:

1. Preheat the sandwich maker and grease with some cooking spray.
2. When the green light appears, place the bottom half of the biscuit in the bottom ring.
3. Top with the cheese, ham, and pepper rings.
4. Lower the cooking plate and crack the egg into it. Season with some salt and pepper.
5. Add the top biscuit half on top and close the appliance.
6. Cook for 5 minutes.
7. Open carefully by sliding clockwise and transfer with plastic spatula to a plate.
8. Serve and enjoy!

Nutrition:

- Info
- Calories 270 Total Fats 15.5g Carbs 14g Protein 17.7g Fiber 0.5g

Almond Pancake With Egg And Prosciutto

Servings: 1

Cooking Time: 4 Minutes

Ingredients:

- 2 4-inch Almond Flour Pancakes, fresh or frozen
- 1 Egg
- 1 ounce chopped Prosciutto
- 1 ounce shredded Cheddar
- Salt and Pepper, to taste

Directions:

1. Preheat the sandwich maker and grease it with some cooking spray.
2. Add one pancake to the bottom ring and top it with prosciutto and cheddar.
3. Lower the top ring and cooking plate, and crack the egg into it. Season with salt and pepper.
4. Add the second pancake on top and close the unit.
5. Cook for 3 minutes or 4 if using frozen pancakes.
6. Open carefully and transfer to a plate.
7. Serve and enjoy!

Nutrition:

- Info
- Calories 430 Total Fats 34.5g Carbs 5.8g Protein 25g Fiber 1.3g

Shaved Asparagus And Balsamic Cherries With Pistachios Panini

Servings: 4

Cooking Time: 6 Minutes

Ingredients:

- 1 to 1 and 1/2 cups pitted, chopped Bing cherries
- zest from 2 lemons
- 3 to 4 tbsp. balsamic vinegar
- roughly 1/2 bunch of thick-stalk asparagus, shaved with a mandolin or vegetable peeler
- 2 tbsp. fresh mint, thinly sliced
- 2 tbsp. fresh basil, thinly sliced
- 2 tbsp. pistachio oil
- 1 multigrain baguette, cut in half, and split open
- ricotta
- fresh mozzarella
- salt and freshly-cracked pepper
- 1/2 tbsp. butter, softened

Directions:

1. Mix the cherries, balsamic vinegar, and lemon zest. Then salt and pepper to taste.
2. Mix the asparagus mint, pistachio oil, and basil in a different bowl.
3. Cut the mozzarella into slices that are 1/3 of an inch thick. Place them on the inside part of the pieces of bread and place the cherry mixture on top of it. Then place the asparagus mixture on top of that
4. Use a knife top spread the ricotta on the inside of the top pieces of bread, and place it on the asparagus mixture.
5. Cook the Panini on medium heat for 5 to 6 minutes, flipping halfway through. The bread should be brown, and the cheese should be melted.
6. Cut the sandwiches in half before serving.

Chili Sandwich

Servings: 1
Cooking Time: 3 – 3 ½ Inutes

Ingredients:

- 2 ounces cooked ground Beef
- 1 English Muffin
- ¼ tsp Chili Powder
- 1 tbsp chopped Tomatoes
- 2 tsp Beans

Directions:

1. Grease your Hamilton Beach Breakfast Sandwich Maker and preheat it.
2. Cut the muffin in half.
3. When the green light appears, add one muffin half with the cut-side down, to the bottom ring.
4. In a small bowl, combine the tomatoes, beans, chili powder, and beef.
5. Top the muffin half with the beef mixture.
6. Lower the top ring and add the second muffin half.
7. Close the lid and cook for 3 to 3 ½ minutes.
8. Open carefully and transfer to a plate.
9. Serve and enjoy!

Nutrition:

- Info
- Calories 320 Total Fats 16g Carbs 28g Protein 15g Fiber 3g

Piña Colada Croissant

Servings: 1

Cooking Time: 4 Minutes

Ingredients:

- 1 small croissant, sliced in half
- 1 Tbsp. cream cheese
- 1 – 2 Tbsp. finely chopped pineapple
- Shredded coconut
- Honey

Directions:

1. Spread cream cheese on both croissant halves. Place one half into the bottom ring of breakfast sandwich maker, cut side up. Place chopped pineapple and shredded coconut on top. Drizzle with honey.
2. Lower the cooking plate and top ring; top with other croissant half. Close the cover and cook for 3 to 4 minutes or until sandwich is warmed through. Open sandwich maker and remove sandwich.

Sausage Omelet With Paprika And Cheese

Servings: 1
Cooking Time: 4 Minutes

Ingredients:

- 1 ounce cooked breakfast Sausage, chopped
- 2 Eggs
- 1 ounce shredded Cheese
- ¼ tsp Smoked Paprika
- 1 tsp chopped Onion
- Salt and Pepper, to taste

Directions:

1. Preheat the sandwich maker and grease it with cooking spray.
2. Whisk the eggs in a bowl and add the onion to them. Season with paprika, salt and pepper.
3. Pour half of the egg mixture to the bottom ring.
4. Top with the cheese and sausage.
5. Lower the top ring and the cooking plate.
6. Pour the remaining eggs into the cooking plate.
7. Close the unit and cook for about 4 minutes.
8. Rotate the plate clockwise and carefully open. Transfer the omelet to a plate.
9. Serve as desired and enjoy!

Nutrition:

- Info
- Calories 371 Total Fats 28.5g Carbs 2g Protein 25.5g Fiber 0.1g

Muffuletta Breakfast Sandwich

Servings: 1
Cooking Time: 5 Minutes

Ingredients:

- 2 slices thick white bread
- 1 slice deli ham
- 1 slice hard salami
- 1 slice provolone cheese
- 1 tbsp. chopped black olives
- 1 tbsp. roasted red pepper, chopped
- 1 teaspoon minced red onion
- 1 clove garlic, minced
- Salt and pepper to taste
- 1 large egg

Directions:

1. Stir together the olives, red pepper, red onion and garlic. Season with salt and pepper and stir well.
2. Preheat the breakfast sandwich maker.
3. Place one slice of bread inside the bottom tray of the sandwich maker.
4. Layer the ham and salami over the bread and top with the olive mixture.
5. Top the olive mixture with the slice of provolone cheese.
6. Slide the egg tray into place and crack the egg into it. Stir the egg gently to break the yolk.
7. Top the egg with the other piece of bread.
8. Close the sandwich maker and cook for 4 to 5 minutes until the egg is cooked through.
9. Carefully rotate the egg tray out of the sandwich maker then open the sandwich maker and enjoy your sandwich.

Quick And Easy Quesadillas

Servings: 1
Cooking Time: 5 Minutes

Ingredients:

- 2 small round tortillas
- 2 slices cooked bacon
- 1 ounce shredded cheddar jack cheese
- 1 tbsp. minced red onion
- 1 tbsp. minced red pepper
- 1 tbsp. BBQ sauce
- 1 large egg
- 1 tbsp. fresh salsa
- 1 tbsp. sour cream

Directions:

1. Preheat the breakfast sandwich maker.
2. Place one of the tortillas inside the bottom tray of the sandwich maker. Brush with BBQ sauce.
3. Break the pieces of bacon in half and place them on top of the tortilla. Sprinkle with cheese, red onion and red pepper.
4. Slide the egg tray into place and crack the egg into it. Use a fork to stir the egg, just breaking the yolk.
5. Place the second tortilla on top of the egg.
6. Close the sandwich maker and cook for 4 to 5 minutes until the egg is cooked through.
7. Carefully rotate the egg tray out of the sandwich maker then open the sandwich maker.
8. Remove the top tortilla and spread with salsa and sour cream. Replace the tortilla and enjoy your sandwich.

Prosciutto And Fig Panini

Servings: 4

Cooking Time: 6 Minutes

Ingredients:

- 8 (0.9-ounce) slices crusty Chicago-style Italian bread
- 4 ounces very thinly sliced prosciutto
- 1 1/4 cups (4 ounces) shredded Fontina cheese
- 1/2 cup baby arugula leaves
- 1/4 cup fig preserves
- Olive oil

Directions:

1. Lightly coat the one side of each piece of bread with olive oil using a brush.
2. Spread the fig preserve on 4 pieces of bread (not on the olive oil side). On the other pieces of bread put a layer of prosciutto, then arugula and top with cheese. Place the fig coated bread on top with the fig side touching the cheese.
3. Cook the Panini on medium heat for 6 minutes, flipping halfway through. The bread should be brown, and the cheese should be melted.

Provolone Baby Mushroom And Caramelized Onion Panini

Servings: 5

Cooking Time: 4 Minutes

Ingredients:

- 2 tablespoons unsalted butter
- 2 tablespoons olive oil
- 1 and 1/2 large onions (or 2 medium) sliced into 1/4 inch thick slices
- 1 tablespoon sugar
- 1/4 teaspoon thyme
- 2 tablespoons minced garlic (I used 1 and 1/2)
- 1 teaspoon Worcestershire sauce
- 8 oz. fresh baby Bella mushrooms, sliced into 1/4 inch thick slices
- 1/2 teaspoon black pepper
- salt to taste
- 1/4 - 1/2 teaspoon red pepper flakes (or more to taste)
- 1 teaspoon flour
- 1/4 cup mushroom broth (or beef broth)
- 2 tablespoons minced parsley
- 5 - 1 oz. slices provolone cheese, cut in half
- 10 slices of fresh French bread
- Olive oil

Directions:

1. Heat a big skillet on medium heat, making sure it's hot before adding any ingredients. Put in the olive oil and butter, and allow the butter to melt. Then put in the onions and allow them to cook for 5 minutes. Mix in the sugar and cook for an additional 15 minutes. Mix in the Worchester sauce, garlic, and thyme, and allow the mixture to cook for 2 more minutes before mixing in the mushrooms. Cook for 10 minutes before mixing in the red and black pepper along with the flour. Slowly mix in the broth 1 tablespoon at a time, waiting until it's been absorbed before adding another. After you've added all of the broth and it's been absorbed, remove it from the heat and mix in the parsley.

2. Place a layer of cheese on 5 pieces of bread, then the vegetable mixture, and then another layer of cheese. Top with the remaining slices of bread. Brush the olive oil on both the top and bottom of the sandwiches.

3. Cook the Panini on medium high heat for 3 to 4 minutes, flipping halfway through. The bread should be toasted, and the cheese should be melted.

Fried Egg And Cheese Bagel

Servings: 1

Cooking Time: 5 Minutes

Ingredients:

- 1 poppy seed bagel, sliced
- 1 ounce goat cheese
- 1 large egg
- 1 teaspoon chopped chives
- Salt and pepper to taste

Directions:

1. Preheat the breakfast sandwich maker.
2. Place half of the bagel, cut-side up, inside the bottom tray of the sandwich maker.
3. Layer the goat cheese on top of the bagel.
4. Slide the egg tray into place and crack the egg into it.
5. Sprinkle the egg with chopped chives, salt and pepper.
6. Top the egg with the other half of the bagel.
7. Close the sandwich maker and cook for 4 to 5 minutes until the egg is cooked through.
8. Carefully rotate the egg tray out of the sandwich maker then open the sandwich maker and enjoy your sandwich.

Corn Bowl With Tomato, Bacon, And Cheese

Servings: 1
Cooking Time: 3 ½ Minutes

Ingredients:

- 1 Corn Tortilla
- 1 tbsp chopped Tomatoes
- 2 Basil Slices, chopped
- 1 ounce shredded Cheddar Cheese
- 2 Bacon Slices, chopped

Directions:

1. Preheat the sandwich maker and grease it with some cooking spray.
2. Add the corn tortilla to the bottom ring, and press it well inside to make it look like a bowl.
3. Add the rest of the ingredients inside.
4. Close the unit and cook for 3 ½ minutes.
5. Lift up to open and carefully transfer to a plate.
6. Serve and enjoy!

Nutrition:

- Info
- Calories 262 Total Fats 16.4g Carbs 13g Protein 16g Fiber 1.9g

Parmesan And Bacon On Whole Wheat

Servings: 1

Cooking Time: 5 Minutes

Ingredients:

- 2 slices whole wheat bread
- 3 slices bacon, cooked
- 2 tablespoons grated parmesan cheese
- 1 large egg

Directions:

1. Preheat the breakfast sandwich maker.
2. Place one piece of bread inside the bottom tray of the sandwich maker.
3. Break the pieces of bacon in half and arrange them on top of the bread.
4. Top the bacon with the grated cheese.
5. Slide the egg tray into place and crack the egg into it. Use a fork to stir the egg, just breaking the yolk.
6. Place the second piece of bread on top of the egg.
7. Close the sandwich maker and cook for 4 to 5 minutes until the egg is cooked through.
8. Carefully rotate the egg tray out of the sandwich maker then open the sandwich maker to enjoy your sandwich.

Southwest Quesadilla

Servings: 1
Cooking Time: 4 Minutes

Ingredients:
- 2 small corn tortillas
- 3 slices avocado
- Sea salt and pepper
- 1 slice tomato
- 1 slice Monterey Jack cheese
- Fresh chopped cilantro
- 1 egg

Directions:
1. Place one corn tortilla in the bottom of sandwich maker. Place avocado on top and sprinkle with sea salt and pepper. Then add tomato, cheese and sprinkle with cilantro.
2. Lower the cooking plate and top ring; crack an egg into the egg plate and pierce to break the yolk. Place other corn tortilla on top and close the lid.
3. Cook for 3 to 4 minutes or until egg is cooked through. Gently slide the egg plate out and remove quesadilla with a rubber spatula. Slice in half and serve.

Spinach Havarti Sandwich

Servings: 1
Cooking Time: 4 Minutes

Ingredients:

- 1 English muffin
- 2 tsp. mayonnaise
- ½ tsp. yellow mustard
- A few baby spinach leaves
- 1 slice Havarti cheese
- 1 egg
- Sea salt and pepper

Directions:

1. Spread the mayonnaise and mustard on both halves of English muffin. Place one half, mayo/mustard side up into the bottom ring of breakfast sandwich maker. Place baby spinach leaves and Havarti cheese on top.
2. Lower the cooking plate and top ring; crack an egg into the egg plate and pierce to break the yolk. Sprinkle some sea salt and pepper on the egg and top with other muffin half.
3. Close the cover and cook for 4 to 5 minutes or until egg is cooked through. Gently slide the egg plate out and remove sandwich with a rubber spatula.

Apple And Brie Croissant Sandwich

Servings: 1
Cooking Time: 4 Minutes

Ingredients:
- 2 Apple Slices
- 1 ounce Brie, crumbled
- 1 Croissant
- 2 tsp Cream Cheese

Directions:
1. Preheat and grease the sandwich maker.
2. Cut the croissant in half and spread one teaspoon of cream cheese over each half.
3. When the green light appears, place one of the croissant halves into the bottom ring, with the cut-side up.
4. Top with the apple slices and brie.
5. Lower the top ring and cooking plate and place the other croissant half inside.
6. Close and cook for 4 minutes.
7. Turn the handle clockwise, open, and transfer to a plate.
8. Serve and enjoy!

Nutrition:
- Info
- Calories 369 Total Fats 23g Carbs 29g Protein 11g Fiber 2g

Ground Beef Sandwich Pitas

Servings: 8

Cooking Time: 10minutes

Ingredients:

- 2 ½ lb. Ground beef
- 1 onion, chopped
- ¾ cup Parsley, chopped
- 1 tbsp. Coriander, ground
- ¾ tsp. Cuminutes, ground
- ½ tsp. Cinnamon, ground
- 2 tsp. Salt
- 1 ½ tsp. Black pepper, ground
- ¼ cup of Olive oil
- 8 thick pita bread, medium, with pockets
- Olive oil to pat the pita bread.

Directions:

1. In a bowl add the ground beef and add ¼ cup of oil, black pepper, salt, cinnamon, cuminutes, coriander, parsley, and onion. Mix well and let it chill in the refrigerator for 1 hour.
2. Preheat the sandwich press on medium.
3. Open pockets in the bread and fill each with the ground mix. Try to fill it to the edges too. Press to seal.
4. Place them on the sandwich maker and cook for 5 minutes without applying too much pressure. Now press and cook for a few minutesutes more. Cook until the meat is cooked well.
5. Serve and enjoy!

Cheesy Chicken Waffle Sandwich

Servings: 1
Cooking Time: 4 ½ Minutes

Ingredients:

- A couple of thin cooked Chicken Slices, about 2-3 ounces in total
- 1 slice American or Cheddar Cheese
- 1 Prosciutto Slice
- 2 tomato Slices
- 2 tsp Mayonnaise
- 2 Frozen Waffles

Directions:

1. Preheat and grease the sandwich maker.
2. Cut the waffles into 4-inch circles so that they can fit inside the unit.
3. Place on waffle on top of the bottom ring.
4. Add the chicken, place the tomato sliced on top, and spread the mayo over.
5. Top with the prosciutto and finish it off by adding the slice of cheese.
6. Lower the top ring and add the second waffle.
7. Close the unit and cook for 4 ½ minutes.
8. Serve and enjoy!

Nutrition:

- Info
- Calories 350 Total Fats 28g Carbs 22g Protein 24g Fiber 2g

Caramel Cashew Waffle Sandwich

Servings: 1
Cooking Time: 3 Minutes

Ingredients:

- 2 small round waffles (store bought or homemade)
- 1 Tbsp. store bought caramel sauce
- 2 Tbsp. finely chopped cashews
- 2 strips bacon
- 1 egg

Directions:

1. Spread caramel sauce on both waffles. Place one waffle into the bottom ring of breakfast sandwich maker, caramel side up. Sprinkle cashews on top, then top with bacon.
2. Lower the cooking plate and top ring; crack an egg into the egg plate and pierce to break the yolk. Top with other waffle.
3. Close the cover and cook for 4 to 5 minutes or until egg is cooked through. Gently slide the egg plate out and remove sandwich with a rubber spatula and slice in half.

Salsa And Shrimp Biscuit Sandwich

Servings: 1
Cooking Time: 3 Minutes

Ingredients:
- 4 small Shrimp, cooked
- ½ tbsp Salsa
- 2 tsp Cream Cheese
- 1 ounce shredded Mozzarella Cheese
- 1 Biscuit

Directions:
1. Preheat the sandwich maker and grease it with some cooking spray.
2. Cut the biscuit in half and spread the cream cheese over the insides.
3. Add one half of the biscuit to the bottom ring, with the cream cheese up.
4. Top with the shrimp and salsa, and sprinkle the mozzarella cheese over.
5. Lower the top ring and add the second biscuit half, with the cream cheese down.
6. Close the unit and cook for 3 minutes.
7. Rotate clockwise and open carefully.
8. Serve and enjoy!

Nutrition:
- Info
- Calories 222   Total Fats 11g Carbs 13g Protein 19g Fiber 0.5g

Ratatouille Panini

Servings: 1
Cooking Time: 16 Minutes

Ingredients:
- 1 red bell pepper, sliced
- 1 tomato, chopped
- 1 clove garlic, minced
- 1 teaspoon dried oregano, or to taste
- salt and ground black pepper to taste
- 1 eggplant, sliced
- 1 zucchini, sliced
- 1 tomato, sliced
- 1 red onion, sliced
- 4 teaspoons olive oil
- 4 slices sourdough bread
- 4 slices mozzarella cheese

Directions:
1. Warm a skillet on high heat, and place the red bell pepper in it for around 5 minutes. The pepper should be soft when it's ready. Place the red pepper, chopped tomato, garlic in a blender or food processor. Blend or process until a smooth sauce is formed. Add salt, pepper, and oregano to taste.
2. Grill the remaining vegetable on a grille or the same skillet for about 6 minutes flipping halfway through. The vegetables will be soft when ready.
3. Brush what's going to be the outside of the bread slices with olive oil. Spread the sauce on what's going to be the inside of the bread. Layer a piece of piece of cheese on 2 of the pieces of bread, then the vegetable mixture, then another piece of cheese. Top with another piece of bread with the sauce side touching the cheese.
4. Cook the Panini on medium heat for 4 to 5 minutes, flipping halfway through. The bread should be toasted, and the cheese should be melted.

Mushroom & Swiss Bagel

Servings: 1
Cooking Time: 10 Minutes

Ingredients:
- 1 multigrain bagel, split
- 2 large mushrooms, sliced
- 1 tsp. butter
- Sea salt and pepper
- 1 slice Swiss cheese
- 1 egg

Directions:
1. Place one bagel half, cut side up into the bottom ring of breakfast sandwich maker.
2. In a small skillet over medium heat, sauté mushrooms in butter until they shrink and begin to let out moisture. Season with sea salt and pepper. Place mushrooms on top of bagel and cover with Swiss cheese.
3. Lower the cooking plate and top ring; crack an egg into the egg plate and pierce to break the yolk. Top with other bagel half.
4. Close the cover and cook for 4 to 5 minutes or until egg is cooked through. Gently slide the egg plate out and remove sandwich with a rubber spatula.

Pancake, Sausage & Egg Sandwich

Servings: 1

Cooking Time: 3 Minutes

Ingredients:

- 2 small store bought or homemade pancakes
- Butter
- 1 sausage patty
- 1 slice cheddar cheese
- 1 egg

Directions:

1. Butter each pancake and place one, butter side up, into the bottom ring of breakfast sandwich maker. Place sausage patty and cheddar cheese on top.
2. Lower the cooking plate and top ring; crack an egg into the egg plate and pierce to break the yolk; top with other buttered pancake.
3. Close the cover and cook for 4 to 5 minutes or until egg is cooked through. Gently slide the egg plate out and remove sandwich with a rubber spatula.

Classic Italian Cold Cut Panini

Servings: 2
Cooking Time: 6 Minutes

Ingredients:

- 1 12 inch hoagie rolls or the bread of your choice
- 1 tablespoon olive oil
- 2 ounces Italian dressing
- 4 slices provolone cheese
- 4 slices mortadella
- 8 slices genoa salami
- 8 slices deli pepperoni
- 4 slices tomatoes
- 2 pepperoncini peppers, chopped

Directions:

1. Slice the rolls in half and then cut it open.
2. Lightly coat the outside of the roll with olive oil using a brush.
3. Brush the inside each piece of bread with the dressing. Then top the bottom pieces of bread with cheese. Add the mortadella, salami, tomatoes and pepperoncini's
4. Cook the Panini on medium heat for 6 minutes, flipping halfway through. The bread should be brown, and the cheese should be melted.

Bacon Cheddar And Tomato Panini

Servings: 4

Cooking Time: 7 Minutes

Ingredients:

- 4 Roma tomatoes, halved lengthwise, pulp and seeds removed
- olive oil
- coarse sea salt
- fresh ground black pepper
- 8 basil leaves, thinly sliced
- 2 tablespoons unsalted butter, melted
- 8 slices sourdough bread
- 8 slices bacon, fully cooked
- 4 ounces sharp cheddar cheese, thinly sliced

Directions:

1. Preheat a small skillet on high heat.
2. Use a brush to coat the cut side of the tomatoes with olive oil and salt and pepper to taste. Put the tomatoes on the skillet with the cut side down. Allow them to cook for 10 to 12 minutes. The tomatoes. Flip the tomatoes about halfway through. The tomatoes should be wrinkly and the tomatoes should be soft to the touch. Check the tomatoes constantly throughout the process so they don't overcook. Once cooked take them out of the skillet and season with basil.
3. Spread the butter on one side of each piece of bread. Place 2 pieces of bacon on the unbuttered side of a piece of bread, then 2 tomatoes and a ¼ of the cheese. Then top with the other piece of bread making sure the butter side is on top.
4. Cook the Panini on medium heat for 5-7 minutes, flipping halfway through. The bread should be brown, and the cheese should be melted.

Feta Lamb And Babba Ghanoush Panini

Servings: 4
Cooking Time: 6 Minutes

Ingredients:

- 1 cup canned grilled eggplant pulp
- 1 small clove garlic, coarsely chopped
- 1 tablespoon tahini (sesame paste)
- 1/2 medium lemon
- Salt
- Freshly ground black pepper
- 2 to 3 sprigs flat-leaf parsley, chopped
- 8 to 12 ounces roasted leg of lamb
- 4 oval pita breads or flatbreads, cut in half horizontally
- 1 to 2 tablespoons olive oil
- 3/4 cup crumbled feta cheese

Directions:

1. Place the eggplant, garlic, 1 teaspoon lemon juice, and tahini in a food processor. Pulse the mixture until it becomes smooth, and then salt and pepper to taste.
2. Slice the lamb into bite sized piece. If you use pita bread use a brush to lightly coat both sides with olive oil. If you're using flatbread just coat one side.
3. Spread the babba ghanoush spread on one side of the bread. If you're using flatbread make sure it's not the side with olive oil. Put the lamb on top of the babba ghanoush, then top with the feta, and finally sprinkle with the parsley. Top with another piece of pita or flatbread. Make sure the oil side is up if you're using flatbread
4. Cook the sandwiches for 4 to 6 minutes on medium heat, and make sure to flip halfway through.

Beef, Waffle, And Egg Sandwich

Servings: 1

Cooking Time: 4 Minutes

Ingredients:
- 1 frozen Beef Pattie
- 2 4-inch Waffles
- 1 Egg, whisked
- ¼ tsp Garlic Powder
- Salt and Pepper, to taste
- 1 slice Cheddar Cheese

Directions:
1. Preheat the unit until the green light appears. Grease with cooking spray.
2. Add one waffle to the bottom ring.
3. Add the beef pattie on top and top with the cheddar.
4. Lower the cooking plate and add the egg to it. Season with salt, pepper, and garlic powder.
5. Close the unit and cook for 4 minutes, not less.
6. Rotate the handles clockwise, lift to open, and carefully transfer to a plate.
7. Serve and enjoy!

Nutrition:
- Info
- Calories 562 Total Fats 38g Carbs 28g Protein 38g Fiber 3g

Beef And Veggies Bagel Sandwich

Servings: 1
Cooking Time: 3 Minutes

Ingredients:
- 1 tsp canned Peas
- 1 tsp canned Corn
- 1 tsp chopped Celery
- 1 tsp chopped Onion
- 1 Tomato Slice, chopped
- 2 ounces cooked Beef Roast, chopped
- 1 tbsp Sandwich Sauce
- 1 tbsp Cream Cheese
- 1 Bagel

Directions:
1. Preheat the sandwich maker and grease it with some cooking spray.
2. Cut the bagel in half and spread the cream cheese over.
3. Place one half of the bagel on top of the bottom ring, with the spread-side up.
4. Top with the beef and veggies, and drizzle the sauce over.
5. Lower the top ring and add the second bagel half inside, with the cream cheese down.
6. Close the lid and cook for 3 minutes.
7. Rotate clockwise and open carefully.
8. Serve and enjoy!

Nutrition:
- Info
- Calories 420 Total Fats 25g Carbs 28g Protein 23g Fiber 5g

Pesto Beef And Mozzarella Panini

Servings: 4

Cooking Time: 5 Minutes

Ingredients:

- 8 slices Italian bread, 1/2 inch thick
- 2 tablespoons butter or margarine, softened
- 1/2 cup basil pesto
- 1/2 lb. thinly sliced cooked deli roast beef
- 4 slices (1 oz. each) mozzarella cheese
- Marinara sauce, warmed, if desired

Directions:

1. Spread the pesto on one side of each piece of bread. Spread the butter on the other side.
2. Split the roast beef between four pieces of bread with the pesto side up and then top with the mozzarella. Place the other piece of bread on the mozzarella with the butter side up.
3. Cook the Panini on medium heat for 5 minutes, flipping halfway through. The bread should be brown, and the cheese should be melted

Cuban Sandwich

Servings: 2
Cooking Time: 10minutes

Ingredients:

- 2 soft sandwich rolls, slice them lengthwise
- Mustard
- 1 dill pickle, sliced lengthwise
- 4 oz. sliced roast turkey
- 4 oz. sliced ham
- 3 oz. Provolone or Swiss cheese
- Softened Butter

Directions:

1. Spread the rolls with mustard. Now layer ½ of the ingredients, cheese, ham, turkey and pickle on each roll. Press them together. Spread the outside with butter.
2. Grill using the Panini for 5 minutes.
3. Serve and enjoy!

Chocolate Donut Dessert Sandwich

Servings: 1
Cooking Time: 5 Minutes

Ingredients:
- 1 chocolate-frosted glazed donut, sliced in half
- 2 tbsp. chocolate hazelnut spread
- 1 ounce cream cheese
- ½ cup sliced strawberries

Directions:
1. Divide the two tablespoons chocolate hazelnut spread between the donut halves, spreading it evenly along the cut edges.
2. Preheat the breakfast sandwich maker.
3. Place half of the donut inside the bottom tray of the sandwich maker.
4. Top the donut with cream cheese and strawberries.
5. Place the second half of the donut on top of the strawberries.
6. Close the sandwich maker and cook for 4 to 5 minutes until heated through.
7. Carefully open the sandwich maker and enjoy your sandwich.

Almond Butter & Honey Biscuit

Servings: 1
Cooking Time: 3 Minutes

Ingredients:
- 1 store bought or homemade biscuit, split
- 1 Tbsp. almond butter
- 1 – 2 tsp. honey
- Dash of cinnamon

Directions:
1. Spread the almond butter on half of the biscuit and then drizzle honey on top. Place biscuit, almond butter side up, into the bottom ring of breakfast sandwich maker. Sprinkle with cinnamon.
2. Lower the cooking plate and top ring and top with other biscuit half. Close the cover and cook for 3 to 4 minutes or until biscuit is warmed through. Remove sandwich with a rubber spatula.

Egg Whites With Mozzarella

Servings: 1
Cooking Time: 5 Minutes

Ingredients:

- 1 thin sandwich bun, sliced
- 1 thick slice tomato
- 1 slice mozzarella cheese
- 2 large egg whites, beaten

Directions:

1. Preheat the breakfast sandwich maker.
2. Place half of the sandwich bun, cut-side up, inside the bottom tray of the sandwich maker.
3. Arrange the slices of tomato and mozzarella cheese over the sandwich bun.
4. Slide the egg tray into place and crack the egg into it.
5. Top the egg with the other half of the sandwich bun.
6. Close the sandwich maker and cook for 4 to 5 minutes until the egg is cooked through.
7. Carefully rotate the egg tray out of the sandwich maker then open the sandwich maker and enjoy your sandwich.

Peach Basil Croissant

Servings: 1
Cooking Time: 4 Minutes

Ingredients:
- 1 small croissant, sliced in half
- 1 – 2 Tbsp. cottage cheese
- 2 tsp. peach jam
- Fresh sliced peaches
- Basil leaves
- Dash of cinnamon

Directions:
1. Spread cottage cheese and peach jam on both croissant halves. Place one half into the bottom ring of breakfast sandwich maker, jam side up. Place peach slices and basil leaves on top. Sprinkle with cinnamon.
2. Lower the cooking plate and top ring; top with other croissant half. Close the cover and cook for 3 to 4 minutes or until sandwich is warmed through. Remove from sandwich maker and enjoy!

Blueberry Marshmallow Sandwich

Servings: 2- 4

Cooking Time: 5minutes

Ingredients:

- 4 slices of sandwich bread
- Butter, salted, at room temperature
- 6 Marshmallows, jumbo size
- ½ cup chocolate chips, white
- ½ cup Blueberries, fresh

Directions:

1. Preheat the sandwich maker.
2. Spread butter on all sides on each slice of bread.
3. Cut the marshmallow in three pieces and place them on the bread slice. Top with chocolate and then with blueberries. Cover with a bread slice.
4. Carefully place the 2 sandwiches on the sandwich maker and press hard.
5. Cook for 2 minutesutes and then flip. Cook for 2 more minutes.
6. Serve as it is or cut in half.
7. Enjoy!

Mexican Gluten-free Pork Sandwich

Servings: 1
Cooking Time: 4 Minutes

Ingredients:
- 2 Corn Tortillas
- 2 ounces pulled Pork
- 2 tsp Salsa
- ½ tbsp Beans
- 1 tsp Corn
- 1 Tomato Slice, chopped
- 2 tsp Red Onion
- 2 tbsp shredded Cheddar Cheese

Directions:
1. Preheat the sandwich maker and grease it with some cooking spray.
2. Cut the corn tortillas into 4-inch circles to fit inside the unit.
3. Place one tortilla to the bottom ring and place the pork on top.
4. Add the salsa, corn, beans, onion, and tomato, and top with the shredded cheese.
5. Lower the top ring and add the second corn tortilla.
6. Close and cook for 3-4 minutes.
7. Rotate clockwise and open carefully.
8. Transfer to a plate.
9. Serve and enjoy!

Nutrition:
- Info
- Calories 360 Total Fats 25g Carbs 21g Protein 24g Fiber 5g

Salmon And Pistachio Melt

Servings: 1

Cooking Time: 3-4 Minutes

Ingredients:

- 2 Bread Slices
- 2 ounces chopped cooked Salmon
- 2 tsp chopped Pistachios
- 1 ounce shredded Mozzarella

Directions:

1. Preheat and grease the sandwich maker with cooking spray.
2. Cut the bread slices into circles so they can fit perfectly inside the unit.
3. Add the first slice to the bottom ring and place the salmon on top.
4. Add the pistachios over and top with the mozzarella.
5. Lower the top ring and add the remaining bread slice.
6. Close and cook for 3-4 minutes.
7. Rotate clockwise and lift open.
8. Transfer to a plate and enjoy!

Nutrition:

- Info
- Calories 423 Total Fats 16g Carbs 41g   Protein 30.8g Fiber 7g

The Ultimate 4-minute Cheeseburger

Servings: 1
Cooking Time: 4 Minutes

Ingredients:

- 1 frozen Beef Patty
- 1 small Hamburger Bun
- 1 slice American Cheese
- 1 ounce cooked and crumbled Bacon
- 1 tsp Pickle Relish
- 2 Tomato Slices
- 1 tsp Dijon Mustard

Directions:

1. Preheat the sandwich maker and grease it with some cooking spray.
2. Cut the bun in half and place one on top of the bottom ring.
3. Add the patty on top and brush with the mustard.
4. Top with bacon, pickle relish, and tomato slices.
5. Place the cheese on top.
6. Lower the top ring and add the second bun half.
7. Close the unit and cook for 4 minutes.
8. Open carefully and transfer to a plate.
9. Serve and enjoy!

Nutrition:

- Info
- Calories 480 Total Fats 31g Carbs 24g Protein 28g Fiber 2g

Bacon Date Sandwich

Servings: 1
Cooking Time: 5minutes

Ingredients:
- 1 French Roll, split in half
- 1 tsp. Olive oil
- 2 oz. Goat cheese, soft
- 3 dates, chopped
- 4 Slices of crisp Bacon

Directions:
1. Brush the bread on the inside with olive oil.
2. On one-half place the cheese, dates, and bacon. Cover with the second half.
3. Press on the sandwich maker for 5 minutes.
4. Serve and enjoy!

Veggie And Pork Mayo Sandwich

Servings: 1
Cooking Time: 3 1/2 Minutes

Ingredients:
- 1 smaller Hamburger Bun
- 1 tbsp shredded Carrots
- 1 tbsp shredded Cabbage
- 1 tbsp chopped Onion
- 1 tsp Pickle Relish
- 1 tbsp Mayonnaise
- 2 ounces chopped cooked Pork
- Salt and Pepper, to taste

Directions:
1. Grease the Hamilton Beach Breakfast Sandwich Maker with cooking spray and preheat it.
2. Cut the hamburger bun in half and brush the mayonnaise over the insides of the bun.
3. Place one of the halves inside the bottom ring, with the cut-side up.
4. Top with the pork and veggies.
5. Season with salt and pepper, and top with the pickle relish.
6. Lower the top ring and add the second half of the bun with the cut-side down.
7. Close the unit and cook for 3 ½ minutes.
8. Rotate the handle clockwise to open.
9. Transfer to a plate and enjoy!

Nutrition:
- Info
- Calories 395 Total Fats 25g Carbs 28g Protein 20g Fiber 1.5g

Eggs Florentine Biscuit

Servings: 1

Cooking Time: 5 Minutes

Ingredients:

- 1 slice multigrain bread
- 1 large egg
- 2 tbsp. plain nonfat yogurt
- ¼ tsp. Dijon mustard
- ½ cup baby spinach
- 1 tbsp. minced yellow onion
- 1 tsp. olive oil

Directions:

1. Heat the oil in a small skillet over medium heat. Add the onion and spinach and stir well.
2. Cook for 2 minutes, stirring, until the spinach is just wilted. Set aside.
3. Preheat the breakfast sandwich maker.
4. Place the piece of bread inside the bottom tray of the sandwich maker.
5. Whisk together the yogurt and mustard in a small bowl then brush over the piece of bread.
6. Top the bread with the cooked spinach and onion mixture.
7. Slide the egg tray into place and crack the egg into it. Use a fork to stir the egg, just breaking the yolk.
8. Close the sandwich maker and cook for 4 to 5 minutes until the egg is cooked through.
9. Carefully rotate the egg tray out of the sandwich maker then open the sandwich maker and enjoy your sandwich.

Breakfast Pizza Sandwich

Servings: 1
Cooking Time: 5 Minutes

Ingredients:
- 2 pieces pita bread, cut to fit sandwich maker
- 2 Tbsp. store bought marinara sauce
- 1 slice ham
- A few slices of pepperoni
- Basil leaves
- 1 – 2 slices mozzarella cheese
- 1 egg

Directions:
1. Spread marinara sauce on both pieces of pita bread. Place one piece into the bottom ring of breakfast sandwich maker, marinara side up. Place ham, pepperoni, basil and mozzarella cheese on top.
2. Lower the cooking plate and top ring; crack an egg into the egg plate and pierce to break the yolk. Top with other piece of pita bread.
3. Close the cover and cook for 4 to 5 minutes or until egg is cooked through. Gently slide the egg plate out, remove sandwich with a rubber spatula and enjoy!

RECIPES INDEX

A

Almond Butter & Honey Biscuit 86

Almond Flour Waffle And Sausage Sandwich 23

Almond Pancake With Egg And Prosciutto 56

Apple And Brie Croissant Sandwich 70

Apple Pie Sandwich 53

Avocado Sandwich With Egg, Ham And Cheese 39

B

Bacon Cheddar And Tomato Panini 79

Bacon Date Sandwich 93

Bacon Egg And Sausage Breakfast Panini 36

Bacon Mozzarella, Zucchini And Tomato Panini 41

Beef And Veggies Bagel Sandwich 82

Beef, Waffle, And Egg Sandwich 81

Blueberry Marshmallow Sandwich 89

Breakfast Pizza Sandwich 96

Buffalo Chicken Panini 35

Buffalo Patty Melt Panini 18

C

Caramel Cashew Waffle Sandwich 73

Cheesy Chicken Waffle Sandwich 72

Chili Sandwich 58

Chipotle Chicken Sandwich 40

Choco-coconut Nut Quesadilla 45

Chocolate Croissant 25

Chocolate Donut Dessert Sandwich 85

Chocolate Hazelnut French Toast Panini 9

Classic Egg, Ham And Cheese 15

Classic Grilled Cheese Sandwich 17

Classic Italian Cold Cut Panini 78

Corn Bowl With Tomato, Bacon, And Cheese 66

Creamy Brie Pancake Sandwich 7

Croissant Sandwich With Sausage, Egg, And Cheddar 16

Crunchy Nutella And Strawberry Bagel 26

Cuban Sandwich 84

E

Egg Whites With Mozzarella 87

Eggs Benedict Sandwich 49

Eggs Benedict With Ham 32

Eggs Florentine Biscuit 95

F

Feta Lamb And Babba Ghanoush Panini 80

Fried Egg And Cheese Bagel 65

G

Ground Beef Sandwich Pitas 71

Ground Turkey Taco Cups 30

Gruyere, Apple And Ham Sandwich 14

H

Ham And Cheese Egg Biscuit Sandwich 55

Ham And Relish Melt 29

Hot Pork Sausage And Srambled Egg Sandwich 8

I

Italian Egg Whites On Ciabatta 54

L

Lemony Delicious Summer Vegetable Panini 38

M

Maple Bacon Waffle Sandwich 21

Mediterranean Sandwich 10

Mexican Gluten-free Pork Sandwich 90

Mexican-style Egg And Beans Sandwich 27

Mixed Berry French Toast Panini 48

Muffuletta Breakfast Sandwich 61

Mushroom & Swiss Bagel 76

O

Olive And Cheese Snack 19

P

Pancake, Sausage & Egg Sandwich 77

Parmesan And Bacon On Whole Wheat 67

Peach Basil Croissant 88

Peanut Butter Bagel Sandwich 42

Peanut Butter Waffle With Banana 20

Pesto Beef And Mozzarella Panini 83

Piña Colada Croissant 59

Pork Sandwiches 11

Pressed Turkey Sandwich 44

Prosciutto And Egg Bagel Panini 33

Prosciutto And Fig Panini 63

Prosciutto And Pesto Panini 12

Provolone Baby Mushroom And Caramelized Onion Panini 64

Q

Quick And Easy Quesadillas 62

R

Ratatouille Panini 75

Red Pepper And Goat Cheese Sandwich 22

S

Salmon And Pistachio Melt 91

Salsa And Shrimp Biscuit Sandwich 74

Sausage & Gravy Biscuit 28

Sausage Omelet With Paprika And Cheese 60

Shaved Asparagus And Balsamic Cherries With Pistachios Panini 57

Smoked Salmon And Brie Sandwich 46

Sour Cream And Crab Cake Sandwich 31

Southwest Quesadilla 68

Spicy Sandwich 52

Spinach Havarti Sandwich 69

Spinach, Parmesan And Egg White 43

T

Taleggio And Salami Panini With Spicy Fennel Honey 34

The Ham & Cheese 37

The Thanksgiving Turkey Cuban Panini 24

The Ultimate 4-minute Cheeseburger 92

The Ultimate Chicken, Spinach And Mozzarella Sandwich 47

Tomato, Egg And Avocado 50

Turkey Salsa Melt 51

U

Ultimate Blt Melt 13

V

Veggie And Pork Mayo Sandwich 94